outdoor living

outdoor living
peter murray

NEW HOLLAND

First published in Australia in 2004 by
New Holland Publishers (Australia) Pty Ltd
Sydney • Auckland • London • Cape Town

14 Aquatic Drive Frenchs Forest NSW 2086 Australia
218 Lake Road Northcote Auckland New Zealand
86 Edgware Road London W2 2EA United Kingdom
80 McKenzie Street Cape Town 8001 South Africa

National Library of Australia Cataloguing-in-Publication Data:

Murray, Peter A. (Peter Allan)
Outdoor Living

ISBN 174 110 150 6

1. Outdoor living spaces. 2. Landscape design. I. Title.

728.9

Design and Production: Peter Murray

My thanks to the following people for their valuable assistance with this book:
Ken Binns, Stephen and Jo from Yardware, Bianca Day, Gabrielle Wells, Bree Howell and Peter Glass, Frank and James from Domo, Justin Doyle, Andrew Smalley, David Kirkpatrick, Kylee Hooker, Neil Turrell, Amander Flaherty, Bruce at Neptune, the gang at Art in Green, Guy Mouritz, Dominique Moloney, Wayne Giebel, Melanie Conomikes and Ashley.

To Gillian—who has inspired me in life and love.
Thank you for your valuable assistance in the preparation of this book.

contents

plan your outdoor living area

Inspiration for your outdoor living area is all around you. Visit open gardens, talk to landscape designers, read landscape and gardening books and look at your surroundings to see what flourishes. Design a garden that will grow with you and allow for simple, inexpensive changes to update your look, such as colour and accessories.

PLANNING YOUR OUTDOOR AREA

Once you have a design concept in your mind for your garden, look at your surroundings. Decide what features you would like to keep and what features you would like to remove. Most garden designers recommend that mature trees, existing walls and established shrubs and plants should remain, and that any new garden design work around these elements. Boundary fence lines, the fall of your land and the sun/shade aspect are also important considerations when drawing up a garden plan, and don't forget to think about how your new garden will fit in with the neighbouring environment.

Before commencing any project it's best to commission a landscape designer to give you a detailed drawing and a list of all the required tasks involved in transforming your garden. It's your choice whether you wish the designer to complete the job from start to finish; or whether you hire tradespeople for the major jobs, which may include walling, paving, the installation of a watering system and any electrical work, and then complete the small tasks yourself. Always check with your local council before beginning any work.

There are a few rules to follow when you start designing an outdoor area. Firstly, note any window views, focal points (including trees, walls and water features) and entertaining areas in your plan and how you want them to be represented in your garden—whether they be paved or showcase a particular plant or ornament. Next ensure the concept and theme of the garden gels with the house for a smooth transition. To avoid the house being segregated from the garden, everything should flow

Above: Potted succulents are perfect for adding texture to any patio or balcony.

Opposite: The owners of this garden approached landscape gardeners to plant their garden after having a design drawn at the completion of the new house. Their builder constructed the retaining walls and stone pitching in keeping with the character of the house.

including the style, colour and texture. A good garden design ensures that the outside of the house, whether it be an outdoor family room or dining area, carries on the style of the interior of the house. Lastly, choose the right plants for your climate and soil conditions. For example, don't plant English box in Queensland or West Australia because it will die! Check how the sun moves around the garden for most of the day and consequently where the shaded areas are. Garden books will advise you on the right selection of plants for either sunny or shaded areas within your garden.

When seeking garden designers or tradespeople to help with the planning and planting of a new garden, ask friends and family for any recommendations and check out your local newspapers. A good piece of advice is to place an advertisement in your local newspaper for a particular trade. It's amazing how quickly people respond. Usually, they have a few days inbetween major jobs and are available for the coming week. You'll have a few people to choose from; the person who you communicate the best with and who can show you examples of previous work is the right choice.

Creating your own tranquil retreat should be exciting and enjoyable. Your garden should be a place that reflects your personality and where you can relax in quiet contemplation or enjoy entertaining family and friends.

In Australia, our homes are designed to take advantage of gardens. Whether you live in a house, a terrace or an apartment, there is always space to create an outdoor area—a sunroom of container plants, floor cushions and book shelves; a backyard of tropical garden beds, water features, Balinese benches and sculptures; or a balcony with French-inspired urns and wrought-iron furniture.

Above: This Balinese wall carving is the perfect accessory for any tropical garden.

Opposite: No tropical garden is complete without a water feature of some kind. This clever design is a combination of a fountain and a pond filled with koi. The water cascades over a tiled wall into the lower reservoir, thus aerating the water and making it healthier for the fish.

Above: The limestone capping on the pool and the steps of this fountain aids drainage while providing a decorative feature of an otherwise plain structure.

Below and opposite: The front courtyard directly outside the kitchen is often used as an alfresco dining area. It overlooks a large water feature filled with koi and papyrus, which adds to the peaceful ambience of the area.

The inspiration for this Moroccan garden started with the magnificent old date palm in the centre of the courtyard. An obvious focal point, the owners then paved recycled brick in a basketweave pattern around it and then constructed sandstone walls to complement the area and support the raised garden beds. Plants such as yucca, agaves (top and bottom) cumquats and mondo grass were chosen for their low water consumption and maintenance. French Moroccan blue outdoor accessories were selected to continue the theme.

The quiet location fully utilises the surrounding lake views with its outdoor living space. The landscape was divided through the middle by a retaining wall that left two unusable spaces connected by a set of steps. A pergola was erected to create entertaining areas that took on the views of the lake. The hedge of gardenias bordering the pergola provides a wonderful perfume when the owners are entertaining.

Previous page: This small, sheltered dining area is perfect for entertaining during summer. The design incorporates a colour scheme that blends in with the beautiful surroundings, particularly the uninterrupted views of the water. Ensuring easy access to the jetty was also taken into consideration.

This outdoor area provides easy access to all parts of the garden and contains low-maintenance plants such as agapanthus (bottom left), rosemary (bottom right) and lilly pillies. The pergola was built on a separate level to create a private outdoor living area that didn't obstruct the view from the house.

plan your outdoor living area • **21**

The open garden room easily takes advantage of its tropical Queensland climate. The design allows two separate outdoor living areas to be incorporated into the landscape. A lush planting of bangalow and golden cane palms, cordylines, and agaves complemented by the vibrant pink of the potted Chilean jasmine, adds to the beautiful surroundings. A water feature and sandstone paving were chosen to add elegance to the design.

Left and below: The idea behind this courtyard design was to bring some life back into the old space which had not had any major work done to it for 25 years. The transformation included paving the area, erecting a low retainer wall with capping to separate the garden bed from the paved area, and adding a water feature to create a calm atmosphere. Note how all the textures and tones perfectly complement each other.

Opposite: Extending the relaxed Mediterranean decor of the interior of the house to the outdoor area was behind the design here. The theme is carried through with the use of similar shaped tiles, a sandstone plant stand and lion fountain, and casual furniture painted in a complementary colour to the surroundings. The garden features pruned roses and Japanese box, both adding a formal flavour.

Above: Any corner of a garden can incorporate texture and form. A slate wall and arched wooden door creates visual interest while providing privacy.

Opposite: A Tuscan garden is stylish, warm and inviting. Aged brick paths, an exquisite Italianate fountain, formal box hedging and the magnificent perfume from lenten roses (top left) captivate the senses in this Mediterranean oasis.

A walkway draped in wisteria between the house and outdoor rooms provides a welcome relief from the summer sun. English box has been used in long planters throughout, and round columns give a stately appearance. The kitchen and entertaining area in the main house open up to the outdoors, providing a relaxed atmosphere for the owners and their guests.

The garden of this home reflects how well established the residence is. Mature gum trees and conifers and an array of shrubs including hydrangeas, arum lilies, ferns, roses, philodendrons and pansies create a garden full of texture and colour. The lush walkway gives the appearance of a never-ending acreage.

A feeling of old world charm is brought to life in this vibrant garden. Beds of azaleas, irises, poppies and Japanese maples were planted to create an oasis of colour in this corner of the garden. The stone walls draped in clematis create a pleasant nook for sitting and enjoying the surroundings.

This garden design was to create a formal atmosphere, but allow better access to the house for visitors and the owners. The main pergola at the base of the front stairs overlooks the pool but has its own water feature set in the garden. The back of the fountain is tiled in high gloss green tiles to reflect the light during the day and night with the aid of lighting. A small courtyard off the kitchen has its own water feature that is modelled from a traditional well. The tiles on this water feature are handpainted with a continuous ivy detail.

outdoor living
is a lifestyle

Large open spaces, blue skies, areas to relax and entertain day or night. Outdoor living is a lifestyle that is
enjoyed throughout Australia. Patio designs range
from rich, bright colours to natural Australian themes
all incorporated into an entertainer's paradise.

A HAVEN TO SUIT YOUR LIFESTYLE

When you have an outdoor living area, you want it to suit your needs and the time you have to maintain it. Basically, its components must reflect your personality and your lifestyle. Do you want the area to act as a retreat from the stresses of everyday life? Do you want a beautiful area to be admired and enjoyed, a place to enjoy your hobbies and interests, or a space for the kids to run around in? If you need time alone, does it need a little nook where you can meditate or take refuge in a good book, while still having the space to hold a party or a barbecue? All this needs to be considered when creating your outdoor living area.

After establishing the purpose of your area for your lifestyle, you need to decide how much time and effort you want to spend looking after the space. Be realistic: it may be fun maintaining it now when everything is new and exciting, but will you get bored later? Will you be able to water the plants regularly and sweep the leaves off the pavers in autumn? Can you afford a gardener if one is required for the upkeep of the landscape? While grass may be perfect for children to play on, will you have the time to do the weeding and mowing that is required to maintain a lawn? Ensure you select drought-resistant and low-maintenance plants if you have little time to tend to your garden.

Once you have decided on what you want in your outdoor living space, design and equip it to suit your tastes. If you want to entertain outside, ensure there is sufficient space for dancing, drinking, a barbecue and of course, furniture for people to sit and eat at. Retaining walls are ideal for creating garden beds and can also act

Above: A swimming pool adds purpose and interest to any garden design and is ideal for people who love swimming or lazing around water during the hot summer months.

Opposite: This entertaining area is perfect for all seasons. The pergola next to the pool provides welcoming shade on hot summer days. The stone blends in perfectly with the contemporary style of the home and the bush outlook.

as a seating area. An awning or pergola provides valuable shade on hot summer days as well as shelter from rain during storms. Pots of flowering plants provide colour and texture to a patio, deck or courtyard. You may prefer to grow herbs such as rosemary, basil and parsley in this area, that are readily on hand for all your cooking needs.

If the area is primarily a place to relax in, then let your imagination go wild and include a hammock to laze in, or sun lounges, mats or cushions to lie on. Plant shrubs such as lavender and jasmine, which provide a wonderful perfume to the surrounds. Position chairs so that they catch the morning sun while you enjoy a cup of coffee and fresh air before work. Install a water feature to help in any meditative reflection you care to enjoy in your private haven. The options are endless.

If you want an area to be active in, then install a swimming pool—even a lap pool will do. Sleek designs can be incorporated into the style of your house and garden. It is important that children are not left unattended near water, so a fence must be considered when installing a pool.

Perhaps you want a garden to showcase a well-tended planting arrangment—a spectacular display of flowers and foliage that reflects your skills as a gardener? A teak bench can always be positioned next to the showpiece, for you to sit and enjoy your creation.

Whatever you decide to put in your garden, make sure you have the time and energy to keep it up to scratch.

Above: Sun lounges are the perfect accessory for lazing around a pool. Comfortable and durable, the many styles available cater to any garden theme.

Opposite: A vibrant palette creates a happy atmosphere in any entertaining area. The use of a solid red colour on the trimmings and walls contrasts beautifully with the sandstone pavers and blue tiles in the pool.

The outdoor area here has the dual function of an entertaining area with a swimming pool. It is a well-used spot during the summer months. The idea was to capture the natural bush setting while at the same time introducing a modern, yet tropical theme—both elements work together wonderfully well. Traditional bark chips have been used as mulch for the beds of Murraya paniculata, *impatiens* and *agapanthus*.

The pool seems to disappear into the natural bush. Large sandstone pavers have been used for the deck area and bull-nose sections of the pool. Simple designs add to the complex location including safety glass panels that allow a full view of the native bushland. The solid, cast-aluminium furniture adds to the modern appeal of this design with the overall space serving as an entertaining area as well as a spot for the family to gather and enjoy warm summer days sunbaking and swimming.

The balcony design allows the owners to feel that they have a garden in a high-density area. Three main elements have been incorporated into the design: colour, privacy and low upkeep. The bright colours of the building exterior, pots, foliage and flowers reflect a bold approach to the design. One of the main concerns of the owners was to screen the balcony from neighbours, but to still allow enough space for them to enjoy the outdoor area. This was achieved by planting weeping lilly pilly close together in ceramic troughs. The lilly pilly will be hedged to create a lush green screen that takes up minimal room. The bougainvillea (below) will be trained up an empty wall in a criss-cross pattern. A potted lime tree provides colour and fresh juice for cooking and drinks.

A contemporary house has been modelled for the owners to allow maximum exposure to the outdoors. The family room and terraced bedroom upstairs enjoy beautiful views of the grounds as well as distant nature reserves. The barbecue area is an entertainer's delight. Skylights open up the area.

A secluded undercover pool lies behind the entertaining area with separate areas for exercising. The sandstone theme has been carried through to lighten the area.

This waterfront balcony was designed for a couple who wanted a low-maintenance, high-impact garden. Two outdoor areas, one for dining and one for relaxation, were created on the large balcony separated by a large water feature. Two weeping lilly pilly with stunning red foliage frame either side of a view of the city. Since maintenance was to be kept to a minimum, plants were selected primarily for foliage interest and salt and wind tolerance. All plants chosen had red- or purple-tinged foliage and/or bark.

A screen of Canary Island strawberry trees and rubber plants blocks unsightly views on one side of the balcony and creates a lush forest feel. The waterfront side of the balcony is bordered with sculptural terracotta pots planted with New Zealand flax to enhance but not block the view of the boats. The table centrepiece is a large ceramic pot filled with succulents such as echeveria. Large glazed Chinese dragon sculptures have been placed on either side of the antique teak bench to give a sense of humour and fun to the otherwise formal balcony.

Give yourself a break from the rigours of everyday life by creating a secluded garden of old-world sophistication and charm. The design here has a restrained and elegant style of antiquity with a modern touch in the plantation shutters, which are framed against the pergola in one of five individual garden rooms. The area is perfect for reading, playing cards and games or just sitting in and reflecting on good times. Virginia creeper has been planted to cover the grey columns and add a little colour, while the garden beds have climbers with delicate flowers such as native violets (right) and blue columbine. The wicker furniture has been painted to match the surroundings.

Above: This sandstone patio is surrounded by hedges of Japanese box and lilly pilly, creating a classic French Provincial atmosphere. The moss on the pavers and pond adds an aged feel to the area, as if the garden has been there for centuries. This secluded spot allows for moments of relaxed intimacy.

Opposite: The rear wall of this pooled area is clad in viburnum and frangipani, flooding the house with fragrance throughout summer. High hedges are an attractive alternative to fences and add privacy to any garden from street level.

Above: A backdrop of lush shrubs and trees blends in with the uncomplicated mix of rustic wicker furniture and shutters, cracked patio flooring, weathered neoclassical columns, climbing roses and colourful nasturtiums. The look is perfect for those who want to sit and enjoy a pleasant vista, and is an attractive entrance to the home.

Opposite: A secluded corner of the garden for quiet contemplation in the natural surroundings. Plants of various shapes and colours were chosen to give a layered effect to the garden beds, with rustic terracotta pots filled with English box framing the wooden bench. The spreading branches of the magnificent bauhinia provides valuable shade on hot days.

design influences

We all have designs in our mind that we would like to replicate in our homes and gardens. It may be from that holiday in Santorini that has always stayed in your memory or a tour through India, France, England or the Pacific Islands. Whatever culture happens to inspire you, it is easy to capture its influence in your outdoor living area.

CREATING YOUR GARDEN STYLE

The theme of your outdoor living retreat needs to be decided on before you begin to furnish it with accessories. First, you need to consider the look you want and whether it will comfortably fit into the actual outdoor space you have, whether it will complement the design of your house and, of course, whether you will ever tire of it. Do you want the space to have a rustic Mediterranean look or a sunbaked Sante Fe feel? Is it to be tropical, minimalist, English cottage or Japanese in tone? Do you want an eclectic mix of cultures or an authentic design of just one? And aside from cultural influences, a particular habitat, colour or fabric can also be the driving force behind your design. When you select all the elements to adorn the area—the flooring, furniture and plants—they must all match your chosen theme.

When selecting a style, ensure that it ties in with the architectural and interior design of your home. If you live in an old Federation house, then choose an outdoor design that will complement this, such as aged bricks for the pathways, wrought-iron garden furniture, and plantings of Federation daisies, English box and David Austin roses. If you live in a modern concrete building that has an industrial feel, then perhaps gravel flooring, metal pots filled with cacti and succulents and sleek perspex or cast-metal furniture will suit.

Once you have chosen the style, carefully pick each element for the best results and take the time to find the perfect accessories for your design. Don't just settle for wooden fencing if a bamboo fence would better suit your Asian retreat. Terracotta tiles will embellish a

Above and opposite: A tropical retreat can be re-created in all parts of Australia. Palms, exotic flowers and outdoor furnishings are a great source for every influence in style, durability and comfort. Bring your family room outdoors. Sofas and armchairs with low tables are perfect to relax in during balmy evenings and will prompt good conversation.

Mediterrean courtyard much better than aged bricks. The key is to make sure that the elements complement each other and that the colours and fabrics don't clash. If you like muted colours, then make sure the flooring, furniture and fabrics all match in tone. If you want to combine different styles, always keep the basic idea in mind. Lastly, whatever design you go with, make sure you have fun completing it.

This setting of finely woven metal is light and doesn't detract from the rustic scenery. Heavily influenced by French Provincial design, the combination of the furniture with the weathered stone paths and stairs and hedges of English box creates a lovely spot to enjoy breakfast. Plantings of lavender (below), climbing roses, wisteria and cyprus can add to the theme.

Wooden decking, tall square pillars, wicker furniture and lanterns conjure up a mood of Asia. A mix of Eastern and Western cultures, pencil pines and exotic palms add to the contemporary design of this outdoor dining area. Texture is added through an assortment of interesting foliage plants, such as yuccas, Copernica palms, erigeron, lavender and daisy bushes. The superb potted aeonium succulent and Japanese fatsia add further visual interest. The design is simple and affordable and can be easily recreated outside your back door.

Clean lines and a strong focus on stonework and decking works particularly well in pool areas. This design is modern and minimalist with an expression of quality. A tropical oasis has been created using a combination of grey, cream and neutral tones for serenity, with exotic palms and select accessories, such as the shaded chair beds, added to complete the look.

The new owners of this opulent residence wanted to renovate the garden to match the tasteful French Provincial interior. The first challenge was to cost-effectively repair a failing retaining wall—then the rest of the transformation could begin. Guests are now enticed to explore one terraced room after the next. Divided with lilly pilly hedging, some bathed in frangipani fragrance, each has its own personality. Continuity is maintained by using natural materials in sympathy with the local environment. The area needs little upkeep, because the materials look better as they age.

planning your courtyard garden

Areas in which to relax and entertain are a must-have, especially in city dwellings. Courtyard gardens are special places. Enclosed by walls, they are sheltered and private and have their own unique urban ambience.

A LITTLE SLICE OF HEAVEN

Courtyard gardens are usually long and narrow or tiny and rectanglar, and often enclosed by a high wall or fence. City dwellers cherish this valuable space as it is often the only outdoor area where they can dry out the washing, entertain friends with a barbecue, allow children to play, store garbage bins, and get a breath of fresh air. When designing a courtyard, make sure it looks just as good from the inside of your house as it does outdoors—it really should be a continuation of the interior design of your home.

A few considerations need to be kept in mind before you start designing your courtyard garden. You need to decide whether it is a place primarily for entertaining, for children to play in, an exercise area with a lap pool, a home for pets, a haven for contemplation or all of the above.

As with all gardens, small or large, the fundamentals remain the same—sunny and shady areas, the condition of the soil and any views need to be taken on board. However, courtyard gardens tend to be more sheltered from the elements, such as wind or frost, so unusual and exotic plants often thrive in these spaces.

Draw a sketch of your property with an idea of your requirements. A landscape designer can then draw the design to scale, knowing what will and won't work, and add a professional touch through their experience starting with the bones—the walls, paving, levels of the land, electrical outlets for lighting and potential water features. For information on plant selection, the landscape designer may include their suggestions on the plan. Visit your local garden centre and explain your soil conditions and discuss your courtyard garden—they will also be able to help you choose the right plants.

This courtyard is easy to maintain and the attached pavilion has added a new dimension to the home. Two levels have been created, each containing lawned areas, with a screen of camellia against the back fence. Box hedging adds a formal touch.

The key to a successful courtyard design is to make it appear bigger than it really is. Mass plantings of your favourite shrubs and flowers give an appearance of a larger area. This works particularly well when thick hedges are used around the boundaries. Select only a few urns, sculptures and pots as focal points, so the area looks uncluttered, and create different levels, such as a raised deck or raised flower beds, to alleviate monotony. A well placed tree stops the space looking flat and containers of colourful flowers scattered around the yard add interest. And lastly, position mirrors in an archway or surrounded by foliage to reflect light and to create the illusion of another garden room.

A major benefit of a courtyard garden is that it is easy to maintain. A tiny garden only requires a little bit of pruning, sweeping and general tidying to bring it back to perfection—but make sure you do this regularly. And because you have fewer plants than most gardens, you will use less water and fertiliser to maintain their health.

The courtyard garden should reflect your personality. It should be a fun process to the end result and extremely gratifying for the soul. Whatever your look—modern, Victorian, traditional—keep the theme simple. Also keep in mind that everything should be to scale with the size of the garden. A large tree will fill the garden with too much shade and a grand statue or water feature will dominate the space. The trick is to use subtle colours, such as light greens, greys, blues and neutrals, that reflect light and add form.

Finally, dress your courtyard with furnishings that match your style. The area will become an alternative outdoor room where you can escape from the hustle and bustle of daily life.

Above: Eclectic pieces collected during overseas travels can greatly add to the theme of a courtyard. Here a stone elephant enlivens a shady corner of an Asian-inspired garden.

Opposite: Brick retaining walls were constructed to give the yard a level area with bright colours contrasted against the steel grey of the planter boxes. A water feature was incorporated into the wall on the opposite side of the pavilion and low voltage lighting was used throughout the garden.

A formal courtyard garden is much loved by those who own an old Federation or Victorian terrace. To re-create a miniature version of the popular gardens of Europe, consider hedges such as Murraya paniculata or English box, potted cumquats, Manchurian pear trees, gardenias and camellias, wisteria hanging over an awning, and, of course, a small lawn. Include small sandstone and iron urns, steel fences and gates, intricate fountains and formal garden furniture in the design. An alternative is to use Australian native species that are drought resistant and tolerant of harsh weather conditions, particularly during times when water restrictions are in place. For example, lilly pilly grows extremely well in hot regions and is an excellent hedge. Check with your local garden centre for growing conditions in your region.

Even the smallest courtyard can offer a retreat from the stresses of daily life, so make it a haven where you can hang out and relax. Link the decor so that colours and textures match. Create extra space by constructing a bench of wood or rendered brick next to a wall and throw colour co-ordinated mats and cushions over the top. Vertical plantings of bamboo or hardy tropical plants create a natural screen for privacy and various grasses and shrubs can soften the edges of paved areas.

This courtyard features a series of retaining walls—some rendered brick and some sandstone—to create interesting levels. The focal point of the area is a grey granite sculpture that can be viewed from any position. Texture is added through various foliage plants, including dracaena, ferns and cordylines.

Most owners of inner-city terraces tend to be young professional couples who require a low-maintenance garden with an entertaining area. To maximise the use of a small space, the area can be predominantly paved using large pavers, leaving narrow beds for planting of lush tropical style plants. A long bench seat is installed allowing maximum seating for entertaining friends, and a water feature provides the relaxing backdrop sounds of trickling fresh water.

The sight and sound of water in a courtyard garden provides a calming effect and helps to mask the traffic noise so evident in city life. A well-maintained water feature includes a pump that circulates the water, keeping it clear, insect-free and oxygenated for plants and fish. There are water features to suit all types of gardens, from sleek rendered ponds to grotto wall fountains.

Most courtyard gardens need seating of some kind. Whatever style you choose to go with, remember that the furniture has to be comfortable and useful and able to withstand the elements. You don't have to buy traditional wooden items either; chairs and other outdoor furniture come in a variety of materials, including wicker, plastic, perspex, metal and stone. Remember to coordinate attractive fabrics with the colour scheme of your garden and ensure that they suit the style of furniture.

The objective of this large, open rooftop terrace was to create a private tropical retreat by combining interesting foliage plants with sandstone paving and a water feature. The space can be used for formal dining and more casual entertaining. The installation of a large curved body of water enhances the tranquil atmosphere of the surrounds. Plantings of cordyline, echeverias (below), yuccas, phormium, agaves, ferns and bamboo keep maintenance to a minimum.

The lush plantings of palms, cordylines, agaves and various grasses provide privacy from the elements. Crafted sitting areas, which are highlighted by downlights under the plants, create a cosy atmosphere. Rich silk fabrics are contrasted with the backdrop of cool greys.

Even the smallest courtyard can contain all that is needed to feel a part of nature. Vertical plantings of evergreen climbers such as lilly pilly, star jasmine, bougainvilleas or passionfruit (above) can be fully utilised for year-round greenery. Seating built into the courtyard wall allows for more space, and lattice is used for total privacy.

The idea behind this courtyard was to screen out the terrace houses at the rear of the property and to provide the sound of water to block out inner city noise. Sandstone detail and porphyry paving blend with the stone floors to keep the flow between outside and in. A tall lilly pilly hedge completely blocks the unsightly back lane while providing a soft walling with texture and nesting birds. Japanese box and mondo grass were used to create a tiered effect. Lighting has been introduced for night use—it is subtle and creates a lovely ambience for outdoor dining.

The brief for this garden was to create a functional and elegant outdoor living room. In particular, the owners wanted a lighter, more inviting space that suggested the compact rear yard was larger than it really was. Coloured cement rendering of the townhouse produced clean lines and a feeling of space, allowing the walls to blend seamlessly with the courtyard's limestone paving. A wonderful place to admire the angular contemporary planting and enjoy an evening meal. Pots include plantings of various Phormium, cacti and succulents for low-maintenance gardening. A lighting system beckons you outside to explore the night and the automatic water system allows more time in the day.

The construction of this garden included a detailed timber pergola, limestone paving, low voltage garden lighting and the use of a matching render for the house and the garden. The cushions complement the blue paint used on the pergola and add a splash of colour to the dominant neutral tones.

decking, paths and steps

For a natural look—perhaps even a bush setting—decking is the way to go. The ideal platform for steep blocks or beach homes, decking is an affordable alternative to paving especially if you are handy with a nail gun!

DECKING, PATHS AND STEPS

Sitting areas, paths and garden steps need not be just paved or concreted. Wood is an attractive and practical alternative that will suit any garden—those both contemporary or old-fashioned in style. The colours and textures of wood easily blend in with any natural environment, and it weathers extremely well.

The most favoured type is pressure-treated wood because of its durability, natural appearance, easy installation and resistence to termites. The ideal types of wood to choose when building a deck are hardwoods such as red cedar or teak. They tend to be rot resistant and age well.

The first step to planning a deck is to decide where it is to go. The obvious site is at the back of the house, but you may prefer it elsewhere in the garden to take advantage of a view or a sunny spot to entertain friends and family. Examine the lie of the land and, if it is level, build your deck using bricks or low sleeper walls for the foundations. Angles make the deck more interesting so make sure you incorporate this idea into the design to avoid creating a boring and simple deck.

Most of the structure can be built using sawn wood, with planed timber used for the decking itself. This will save enormously on costs. Most of the fixings can be made with galvanised nails, although coach bolts should be used to assemble the framework with raised decks. And remember to treat all the cut ends and joints with preservative, again to avoid the wood rotting.

This large timber deck was constructed to match the structure and colour of the house. Raised boxed areas allow for extra seating—just throw down a few cushions!

Using timber to create paths and steps in your garden is easy and effective. Paths can be constructed with long planks or with roundels cut across the log and laid like circular pavers. Planks are best to use on straight paths, while roundels work well for curved paths.

The best way to lay a planked path is to first excavate the area to a depth of 100mm and then put down a layer of fine gravel. This will make the planks easier to bed and help drain any water away. Then simply lay down the planks, butting them together and securing them with wooden pegs at regular intervals.

Roundels should be set in concrete to stop them from working loose. To lay roundels, excavate the path area to a depth of 150mm, put down a layer of fine gravel and hammer down the roundels, making sure they butt together and are level, to avoid people tripping when they use the path.

Planks can also be used to make steps in the garden. Simply position them in place to follow the slope of the ground, mark the direction of the path in the bank, and excavate the step shapes into it. Next cut the planks to the width of the path, peg a vertical riser at the back of each step and then lay the treads. Ensure each plank is level across the width with a slight slope towards the front, then secure the plank with long wooden pegs. If you want to use roundels, you will need to cut the steps into the bank deep enough to take pieces cut to 150–200mm. Peg the vertical planks in place first to form the front edge of each step, then position and concrete the roundels that form the tread of the step.

The look of timber is warm and relaxing. Most bleach with the sun to silver if left natural. Wooden decking allows you to create tiers of rooms which add interest. Garden boxes, stairs, seating and planters can be constructed to match your decking using the same materials.

All the timber used in this outdoor area is a high quality treated pine that will withstand termites and age well with the elements. The deck was designed so that the sub-floor of the upper deck was lined underneath to create a roof covering for the living area below. The stairs were designed to be unobtrusive and lead to the pool area.

Above: The rich colour of the wooden decking perfectly complements the teak of the outdoor setting, creating an atmosphere ideal for entertaining.

Opposite: As this rural property was steep and had a natural bush surround and views, decking was used to create an outdoor room that took advantage of the landscape. The blue-grey colour of the trunks of the jacaranda tree and eucalypts was replicated to blend in with the environment. The striking foliage of the trees also contrasts beautifully with the blue-grey of the woodwork.

yardware and outdoor furniture

Yardware accessories influenced by European designs are now abundantly available in Australia. Create a formal or casual entertaining area in your garden and outdoor room using garden furniture and ornaments.

THE FINISHING TOUCH

Garden furnishings and ornaments are much sought after for any home and add the finishing touch to any garden design. Timeless and formal accessories are readily available so visit your local gardening centre or an outdoor furniture specialist to see what is on offer. Choose from water features that blend with the environment, rustic teak furniture settings with matching market umbrellas, magnificent pillars of stone, quaint birdbaths, sundials and lanterns and large earthenware pots.

To make your outdoor room comfortable and inviting, you need to include furniture to laze around in or use for entertaining. Even the smallest garden or patio can house some kind of furniture, whether it's a stool on a balcony, a hammock strung between two trees in a courtyard, solid teak furniture next to a built-in barbecue, or sun lounges by the pool on a large estate.

Select furniture that matches the style of your outdoor living area—Balinese teak benches for tropical gardens, stone tables or cast aluminium settings for French Provincial retreats, metal or perspex chairs for minimalist landscapes. For small areas, built-in furniture is an excellent space-saving option, so think ahead when you are planning any construction work in the garden and request that any rendered walls be built as benches. Custom-made mats and cushions will complete the look and can easily be removed if there is a threat of rain. If you have limited space, purchase folding furniture that can be quickly stored away when not in use. And use furniture for dual purposes; tables can be used not only to eat from, but to display your favourite potted plants or as an area to do the actual potting on.

Above: Lanterns are an easy way to add atmosphere and light to your garden and come in many styles and sizes. They can be suspended from doorways or tree branches, positioned along pathways, or act as centrepieces on tables.

Opposite: This majestic earthenware urn framed by the columns of a pergola is a striking focal point in this garden. It is a dramatic way to make a design impact, while keeping in tune with the Mediterranean style of the outdoor space.

Paint furniture and furnishings to match the colour palette of the flowers and shrubs in your garden, or to work with the theme you want to create. A barbecue setting painted a sand colour works wonderfully in a seaside-inspired garden; metal pots painted white and pale blue complement a shabby chic look.

Sculpture and other artworks look superb in gardens and work to complement your overall theme. Sculptures provide focal points at the end of a vista or path, or can be used as an element of surprise in a hidden corner of a courtyard. Birdbaths and sundials also work brilliantly if they fit the setting. Most are traditional in style, however, so really only suit formal gardens.

Living sculptures in the form of topiary have gained popularity in recent years. They give an added dimension to formal gardens and a sense of elegance. Clip plants such as English box or lilly pillies into a desired shape—whether that be a ball, cone or animal shape.

Obelisks and urns can also be used as focal points in a garden and tend to age well. Many can be purchased with a mottled patina surface to simulate age and use. Wall art such as murals, mosaics or plaques also add visual interest to any blank canvas. You can make your own designs or commission an artist to create what you want. Trompe l'oeil (an artform of illusion) is a great way of making a small backyard look bigger. Imagine an open door leading down a flight of steps into a beautiful Tuscan-inspired garden, or maybe stunning views that just go on and on painted on a flat, boring brick wall. The possibilities here are endless.

Just make sure that whatever accessories you place in your outdoor room are weatherproof, and have sufficient space around them to make an impact.

Above: Formality can be blended with the contemporary. The example above shows the use of modern colour (indigo blue) matched with rustic accessories and objets d'art.

Opposite: Simply elegant is the best way to describe this beautiful setting. To re-create this Mediterranean scene all that is required are low box hedges and paved bricks with the focal point being the urn. The weeping willow adds an element of romance into the design.

The ideas for focal points are endless—formal water features in limestone, rustic recycled brick paving, handmade sculptures and sundials that look like they've been around since Leonardo da Vinci's time. The charcoal shutters behind the featured urn allow the sandstone to come forward. Wisteria makes its way around the pillars and English box hedges give strong perspective from a distance.

Formality can have a Mediterranean feel, the trick is to balance all the elements—particularly the plantings and scultures used—and include rich Mediterranean colours, such as terracotta and blue azure.

Chic cast-metal furniture mixed with Roman columns and urns creates a formal dining setting in this outdoor area. The look is simple to achieve—clean lines, formal plantings such as conifers, box and agapanthus, and traditional water features and sculptures add to the garden's formal appeal.

Accessories enliven any garden, courtyard or patio. Look for handcrafted reproductions that complement your garden theme. Add wall plaques as a feature, purchase functional and attractive furniture and position quirky items, such as bird tap heads or animal sculptures, throughout that add a sense of humour or elegance to the area. The idea is to take the indoors out and match traditional designs with modern pieces.

creative garden
lighting

Garden lighting extends the amount of time you can enjoy your outdoor area. Lighting also helps to bring out the exquisite outdoor charm of your garden—the special elements that make up the area, such as specimen trees and shrubs, sculptures, urns, water features, or mosaics.

LET THERE BE LIGHT

Get the light right, not only because landscape lighting makes it easy and safe for you to walk through your outdoor areas after dark, but also because well-lit entrances, driveways and paths are welcoming. They also allow for identification of visitors and dampen the spirit of trespassers. Light up steps, stepping stones and passageways between buildings for added safety.

Illuminating areas for safety and security, and drawing attention to important features in your landscape, is important. Remember, you should have people in mind when you think of landscape lighting and/or design. When your garden entertaining area is lit up, it can create a mood for the evening.

It is also ideal to use indirect lighting in landscape lighting, not direct 'head-on' lighting, because this tend to deaden the garden at night. Indirect lighting is achieved when the light source is hidden from view. The result is that only the lighting effects are seen. To create intrigue and interest, illuminate certain features, such as an urn, a water feature or an entry pathway. Move lights around to find where they create the most mood and atmosphere.

There is a variety of lights for different effects available. Most nurseries and hardware outlets stock a large range of options, so start exploring. Check out spotlights, recessed wall and floor lights, downlights, bollard lights, pendants and, of course, candles. If the light fixture will be visible in daylight, look for attractive designs that match the style of your garden. An antique lantern won't work in a modern, minimalist garden, for example.

You can create silhouettes by lighting objects from one side, and also emphasise the form of the objects, or plants,

Above: Candles offer perfect mood lighting for evening entertaining.

Opposite: The courtyard takes on a whole new look once darkness falls. Up-lights positioned under specimen trees and flowering shrubs highlight their beauty in the evening.

you are illuminating. The best forms of silhouette-lighting are achieved by either lighting the background—for example, a fence or wall—so the dark object is viewed against an illuminated surface; or by back-lighting the object so that it is viewed against a dim backdrop. When you light an object from opposite directions, it is called cross-lighting. Lights are used either from front to back, or side-to-side.

For the best lighting results, make sure that light fixtures are positioned near the ground, and that the intensity of light from light sources is diverse. Most importantly, if you wish to use indirect lighting to highlight interesting features of your plants, the texture, size and growth habit of them should be taken into account. It is best to consider up-lighting for plants that are full. Also, think of cross-lighting at sharp angles for thick foliage.

Spectacular effects can be created by illuminating water. Fountains look magical when glittering in the dark and floating candles look pretty as they flicker in a bowl or pond. Underwater lights give a celestial ambience and emit a spectrum of wonderful colours.

Always employ a professional electrician to install garden lighting, especially if there is water involved or the possibility of hitting a cable. You'll have peace of mind knowing that the lights will function correctly and there will be no risk of electrocution.

Above: A spotlight accentuates the texture and curves of this gorgeous urn filled with echeveria.

Opposite: This award-winning lighting design illuminates an impressive entrance flanked by two formal squares of box hedging and mature trees. A perfect balance.

The pool complements the angular design of the house and provides privacy from neighbours. The original site was a small area of rock garden and lawn—a generally wasted and unused area. The pool is the focal point of the outdoor area and looks spectacular both night and day. The design has created a visual and recreational asset and incorporates a series of cascades that spill down the weathered granite exterior of the pool, creating a magnificent water feature for the front of the house. The pool's interior is tiled with blue Italian glass mosaics, which allow a generous amount of light to reflect off the surface. The lights also accentuate curves of the pool. The cascade is faced with weathered granite and the balance tank is lined with river stones. The pool is totally elevated and its shape is based on a quarter circle. The pool and adjacent entertaining areas were paved with Hinuera stone from New Zealand. Glass fencing was incorporated into the design to minimise the interruption of views from the house and adjacent entertaining areas.

Above: Spectacular effects can be attained by illuminating water. Fountains look superb glittering in the dark, so try to place spotlights beneath or beside trickling water.

Opposite: Grey and charcoal give a monochromatic theme. Paving with different sized pavers creates a parquetry-type effect. The pebbled wall fountain is illuminated with underwater spotlights, creating a subtle lighting effect that adds to the overall feel of the simple and understated garden design.

As evening falls the garden comes to light. Downlights positioned beneath the urns and pots accentuate their contours at night, giving this garden an air of grace. The pool is a focal point no matter what the time of day or night.

Above: This water feature has been built in front of a mirrored wall to create the illusion of a floating partition between two garden rooms. The superb copper-coloured tiles add to the mirror effect and add warmth to the area.

Opposite: Up-lit standard trees form a border to this reflection pond. Underwater lighting can give an unearthly air to any garden design, so experiment with different colours to achieve your desired ambience. The incorporation of outdoor lighting is best done at the planning stage.

At night, the entertaining area comes alive and the extensive use of downlights, spotlights and garden lighting enhances the surrounds. Every aspect of the home has been highlighted in this grand manor.

designing your **pool** and water feature

Pool designers have a diverse range of designs on offer to suit individual requirement—summer pools, spas, lap pools, water features, ponds or just a simple stream. Pool accessories are endless—glass tiles, specialised cappings, water jets—here are some examples to whet your appetite.

MAKING A SPLASH

Water adds another dimension to an outdoor living area. It's a marvellous way to enliven a dull spot. Reflections in still pools increase the light in a garden and consequently the feeling of space. Water features with moving water help to drown out the sounds of bustling city life and have a soothing effect on the soul. They are perfect for city courtyard gardens. Informal ponds encourage wildlife to come to your garden, such as frogs and birds, or you can incorporate fish, such as koi or carp, into it. Water helps you to relax and unwind, so for any garden retreat it is a must.

Just imagine the delightful feeling of relaxing in your own pool, and floating on its calm waters. It brings you a rare degree of equanimity, a blissful state of self-hypnosis. Water soothes and drives away any qualms and frustrations and your muscles relax making you ready to face each new day of your life with renewed verve and drive.

When you opt to build a simple pool, you need to select a shape, size and 'appearance' that will complement your garden design. The designs are endless and range from the traditional rectangular pool that works well in formal gardens to state-of-the-art tropical paradise pools that can blend in beautifully in a Balinese-inspired retreat.

To design your own pool, map out the area, decide what necessary amenities you require including an outside shower, adjacent change rooms and bathroom, or perhaps an outdoor dining area and shaded area to retreat from the sun.

Courtyard gardens can enjoy the delights and vitality of a pool. It doesn't have to be an olympic-sized swimming pool—a lap pool will do. Plants chosen to adorn the area can have a vertical growth habit such as pencil pines. Trees that have lower branches removed (this is called 'pleaching') will

The pool was designed so that there was easy access to it from the centre of the house. The pool interior is fully tiled to create a cool look that reflects a generous amount of light to brighten the whole area. Twin espaliered pear trees are a feature on the main wall, which was created for privacy. There is plenty of space around the pool for outdoor furniture to be positioned for entertaining or to laze about on hot summer days.

allow for more space and at the same time provide shade and provide privacy from the neighbours.

Ponds give a tranquil effect to a garden. Whether it be a basin with still water with water lilies or an old stone sink filled with aquatic plants, the ideas are endless. A shallow pebble pond lined with river pebbles and cobblestones is easy to make and maintain. You can have one in the garden or on a terrace or patio. Instant pond kits can be assembled quickly and positioned anywhere. Make sure the waterproof liner is not visible around the edges or the effect will be lost.

Fountains have a majestic charm all of their own. Producing moving water effects from fountains—from gushing spouts and bubbling springs to foaming jets and sparkling streams—they add a special ambience to any garden design. All you need is a submersible electric pump to get the water circulating. Fountains come in many shapes and sizes, so visit a garden centre to see what selection is on hand. Lots of small holes produce a spray, while larger ones make jets of water. A fountain head can also be a feature on its own. Cherubs and lion heads are popular in Mediterranean and classical style gardens and there are many cutting edge designs for more modern gardens.

Opposite: This simple design includes a pool area with a dining setting. The formal and balanced garden of ficus trees, box hedges and espaliered pears matches the clean lines of the pool.

A fine pebble floor has been used in this pool while Castlemaine slate provides a natural look around it. The pool has a beach area with rocks strategically placed to create a tropical look. Palms have been planted to provide more shade as they mature.

Opposite: A luxurious cabana is the feature of this outdoor setting. A formal approach has resulted in rows of English box highlighted with water features and antique urns that have been under-lit.

Above: Side-lighting within the steps of the lap pool provides yet another dimension to the area. Outdoor sun lounges and a dining setting have been chosen to complement the colours of the surrounding area.

The pool in this large property was designed to fit in with the surroundings. Natural bush, rocks and plantings create the essential atmosphere. A small pond was also designed and constructed alongside the main pool.

The pool was designed for a large family and has an accompanying entertaining area. The interior of the pool is tiled with glass mosaic, which reflects a spectrum of light into the whole area. The pool was constructed to fit with the large residential home.

Above: A pool can be built at any height. Here the owners can enjoy views of the neighbourhood while taking a dip.

Opposite: The owners required a 20-metre long pool for exercise purposes with an additional request that it look spectacular day and night, summer and winter, and that it be suitable for their young children. The existing site was long and narrow with a number of large existing trees to be incorporated into the overall design. The new landscape integrates seamlessly into the existing formal landscaped areas of the property. A reinforced concrete and beam shade pavilion is a focal point at the far end of the pool. The columns of the shade pavilion extend up out of the water, ensuring that it is visually integrated with the pool and landscape. The pool interior is painted with a custom-made colour and the waterline is tiled with Italian glass mosaic tiles. The areas surrounding the pool are paved with Himalayan sandstone, which extends below water level on the pool steps and water play areas.

This pool was designed with a Balinese feel to tie in with the relaxed contemporary, tropical Asian style of the house. Even though transposed into a bushland setting, the pool harmonises beautifully with its surroundings. The existing large scribbly gums were retained and the pool was carefully designed around them. The pool was elevated and an infinity edge utilised to create the illusion of the water spilling into the bush beyond. A Balinese shade pavilion was created to provide respite from the elements with the columns extending down into the water. The blue-green colour of the water ties in with the surrounding bushland whilst beautifully reflecting the pavilion and adjacent trees.

This contemporary, simple and elegant pool was designed to tie in with the existing house. The feature wall, fountains and water play area is integral part of the pool design. The wall has been faced with the same travertine that has been used around the pool and features spectacular night lighting. The owners wanted the pool to be a visual feature as well as for exercise and entertaining. The site was a very difficult one, with extreme changes in level. The existing residence required partial underpinning to enable the pool and adjacent entertaining areas to be maximised on what was a very steep site. The internal finish of the pool is a blue Italian glass mosaic tile. Travertine tiles were used for the pool surrounds, stairs and balconies. Glass fencing was used on the pool concourse level and stainless steel posts with stainless steel wires were used on the upper balcony level. A variety of evergreen tropical and exotic plants were chosen to provide year round colour, texture and to be able to withstand the poolside conditions.

Above: This contemporary, layered fountain blends in perfectly with the pool design. A simple yet effective mosaic of river pebbles bordered by plantings of dracaena and phormium creates an interesting feature wall.

Opposite: The owners of this home wanted a pool and spa that would take advantage of the ocean views from the rear of the property. They desired a pool that would serve as both a visual and recreational feature—one that would look magnificent day and night. The pool features a unique serpentine shape and is cleverly integrated with the adjacent extensive poolside entertaining areas and landscaped gardens. The design consists of three levels; the highest level is the shade pavilion and spa. Water cascades from the spa level down sandstone steps into the pool and from there cascades into the balance tank set in the lower garden. From the interior of the pool the water appears to spill over into the ocean. Glass fencing was incorporated into the design to minimise the interruption of views to the ocean. Extensive underwater and landscape lighting was designed to create a relaxed yet spectacular effect at night.

The objective for this area was to create a shade structure where the owners could relax near the pool and enjoy a water feature as a focal point of the main outdoor dining area. Integrating rendered concrete block walls onto the sides of the pool allowed the existing sleeper walls to be taken out of play and to also create a wider garden space beside the pool.

This pool was designed and constructed with a wide mosaic ledge as a bar area where the owners and guests can sit in the pool with a drink and place glasses and bottles at a comfortable height close by. The water feature provides a focal point for the main outdoor living area consisting of two ponds at different levels. This makeover now allows the owners to fully relax and unwind and they can entertain family and friends in either formal or informal outdoor living areas. Note how the furniture and rendered walls match the colour of the mosaic tiles perfectly, tying the whole look together.

No pond is complete without some form of aquatic planting. There are many varieties of water plants to choose from, such as exquisite water lilies, horsetail rush, arum lilies, water irises, umbrella grass, club rush, skunk cabbage and variegated water grasses, and they all thrive in water.

A totally new environment has been created for this home. Several levels have been introduced to the design, which has a natural water pond as its main feature. The traditional pond is a mix of slate and concrete and features four male heads all with different facial expressions; adding a touch humour to the design. Beautiful surroundings and established trees have helped to make this outdoor entertaining area a delight for the owners.

The owners of this home have captured the style and romance of Tuscany with their formal approach. The pool is surrounded by antique brick paving with a slate bullnose. Small diamond pieces are added to give a tessellated feel to the area. A large outdoor room has been built to provide visitors with a separate area from the house to relax and enjoy the surroundings.

outdoor living
Picture credits

Photographers
Light On Landscape/Peter Clarke: 128–129, 130, 132, 133, 136, 137, 138–139, 141, 142, 143
Peter Glass & Associates: 134 (Greg McBean), 159 (Phil Aynsley), 160, 161, 162, 163 (Karl Sharp),
Ritz Landscaping: 8, 9, 10, 11, 12, 13t, 13b, 14, 15t, 15b, 25t, 25b
Wayne Giebel Landscapes: 2, 16–17, 18–19, 20, 21t, 22, 23t, 166, 167, 168, 169
Turrell Building Services: 2, 6–7, 38, 39, 40, 43
New Mode Landscapes: 74–75, 76, 77t, 78, 80l, 81, 104, 107, 108–109, 113t (Ken Binns)
Secret Gardens of Sydney: 82, 83l, 83r, 85l, 86, 87, 88, 89t, 89br, 90, 91b, 92, 93t, 93b, 94, 95, 96, 97b, 112 (Ken Binns)
Samara Design: 46, 47t, 52, 53, 54, 55 (Melanie Conomikes)
Art in Green: 34, 35, 36, 56, 57tl, 57tr, 58, 59t, 59b, 72, 73t, 73b, 89bl, 98, 99t, 99b (Ken Binns), 100, 101, 102, 103, 140
Domo Collections: 62, 64, 65, 66, 67t, 68t, 69, 70b, 71, 84, 85tr, 85br, 131
Neptune Swimming Pools: 144–145, 146, 147t, 147b, 148, 150, 151t, 151b, 152, 153154, 155,156, 157t
Yardware: 114–115, 116, 118, 119, 120l, 121, 122t, 122b, 124b, 125, 126, 127tl, 127bl
Toop & Toop: 24, 26, 27r, 28, 30, 31, 48, 49, 50, 51, 174, 175
Outdoor Creations: 27r, 170, 171, 172, 173
New Holland Image Library: 21bl, 21br, 23b, 27l, 29, 32, 33, 41, 42, 45, 47b, 57b, 60, 61, 67b, 68b, 70t, 77b, 79, 80r, 91t, 97t, 113b, 117, 120r, 124t, 127br, 149, 157b, 158

(t = top, b = bottom, l = left, r = right)

Garden designers and landscapers
Turrell Building Services: www.turrell.com.au, (02) 9651 4441
New Mode Landscapes: www.newmodelandscapes.com, (02) 9526 7106
Secret Gardens of Sydney: www.secretgardens.com.au, (02) 9314 5333
Samara Design: 0418 992 354
Art in Green: www.artingreen.com.au, (02) 9807 2677
Domo Collections: www.domo.com.au, (08) 8361 7388
Peter Glass & Associates: www.peterglass.com.au, (02) 9906 2727
Light On Landscape: www.lightonlandscape.com.au, (03) 9824 2050
Nepture Swimming Pools: (03) 9870 5282
Ritz Landscaping: www.ritzlandscaping.com.au, 0404 064 004
Wayne Giebel Landscapes: (07) 3271 3092
Yardware: www.yardware.com.au, (02) 8353 3882
Outdoor Creations: www.outdoorcreations.com.au, (03) 9455 0050
Toop & Toop: www.toop.com.au, (08) 8362 8898